D1561367

GOING TEXT

MASTERING THE POWER OF THE COMMAND LINE

BRIAN SCHELL

Written and designed by:
Brian Schell
brian@brianschell.com
Version Date: July 25, 2018

ISBN-10: 1718641990
ISBN-13: 978-1718641990

Printed in the United States of America

CONTENTS

INTRODUCTION

GETTING TO A COMMAND LINE

USING THE COMMAND LINE:
THE TOOLS

USING THE COMMAND LINE -
THE APPS

ADVANCED TOPICS

INTRODUCTION

Windows. MacOS. Gnome. GUIs (Graphical user interfaces) have been the mainstay of home and office computers for nearly 25 years. Before that there were DOS and the Unix command lines. For most users, the mouse and the attractive, colorful user interfaces offered were more intuitive and easier to learn that the cryptic keyboard commands needed to do most tasks on text-based interfaces. For most people, GUIs are still the best way to go. Still, many of us want more performance, more efficiency, and (arguably) less complexity that can only be found through the keyboard.

This book focuses on getting as much as possible done through non-graphic, non-mouse means. This means the keyboard and the text-mode screen. This means working from the command line and through text-based, non-graphical interfaces. It could mean working with older hardware, but it doesn't have to. Whether you're running on the newest I9 processor, a Mac, iPad, Android phone, Raspberry Pi, or some kind of remote terminal, you can make this happen. Actually, the flexible hardware options are just one more reason to make this switch. Can you make the switch from a $2000 Apple laptop to a $35 Raspberry Pi? Well... *maybe*. This book is here to help you find out. Even if it turns out in the end that you don't want to totally switch to text *exclusively*, the tools and tricks you learn here can still be used from within a terminal in any GUI system.

So what do I mean by "Going Text" in this context? This means we'll be working from a command line, using text-based Unix/Linux-based software. We're going to almost entirely quit using the mouse. We'll be using these command line tools from within Windows, MacOS, or Linux terminal apps, or on other devices by using a terminal program logged into a remote server. As I wrote this book, my alternate titles were "Going Command Line" and "Going Terminal." The final product is a bit of a mash-up of all three ideas.

WHY DO THIS?

Why would anyone want to give up the mouse? Why would anyone want to give up high-resolution graphic screens with pictures, pretty fonts, detailed images, and easy point-and-click menus? Didn't the computer industry just spend 30 years getting us into the world of window-based operating systems and GUI goodness?

Well, there are a couple of good reasons:

- First and foremost, because it's fun. In this age where minimalism and austerity are popular movements, getting things done with less is not just an enjoyable hobby, it can be a constructive challenge. Nothing matches the joy of realizing that you gave up an eighteen-hundred-dollar MacBook Pro for a thirty-five dollar Raspberry Pi and haven't noticed much difference in getting your work done, or better still, find you are getting more done, faster.
- It is usually faster. Oftentimes, we associate text modes with slowness, probably because when we

last ran some of these tools, the computers topped out at 16mHz. It's not like that anymore-- I mentioned a cheap Raspberry Pi in the previous paragraph, but that's not a requirement. I'm writing this using the text-based app Vim on my Lenovo Yoga 910-- a modern laptop with a Kaby Lake i7 processor, 16 Gigs of RAM, and an SD drive loaded with Ubuntu Linux instead of Windows. Minimalism is fun, but sometimes blazing power is even more fun.

- But that's not really what I meant by speed. You can run these tools on darned near anything, but the real speed comes from using the keyboard-only for most tasks. Yes, the mouse is usually easier to learn, but it really slows you down when you have to get work done. Click on this window, select that check box, then click OK, and then maybe click back on what you were doing to get back to work. It's only a few seconds, but all that mousing and clicking counts up. The mouse is strictly optional in the world of text, and often discouraged. Sometimes, learning all those keyboard commands can seem daunting, but it really is faster in the long run.
- The software is generally completely free, and legally free at that. Unless you have some very special proprietary software in mind, everything I am going to show you is open-source under the GPL license or similar license. That's not to say nothing will cost money-- there are still cloud services, remote servers, and possibly subscriptions to services that you find

indispensable. The software, on the other hand, won't cost anything.

- It works. I won't say there are never crashes in the world of text, but it's rare. There's often less to break with a text interface. Besides that, many of the tools we're going to look at have been in regular use for literally decades. Any bugs they ever had were solved long, long ago.

- It's reliable and very customizable. Most apps use simple text files for configuration, so you can get in there and change anything and everything yourself. When you have everything configured exactly the way you want it, you can back up those configuration files easily and restore them if you need to. Not everything, but most apps, save work in straightforward text-based files that can be read by other programs and on any operating system in the future. If, in forty years, you need to access your work, then you'll still be able to get into it. Computerized text has been around since the 1950s, and it's never going to go away.

HARDWARE AND NOTES ON GETTING STARTED

As with everything involving computers, what you can do and how you do it is often based around what kind of equipment you have, and Going Text is no different. First of all, let me say this: you can do almost everything in this book with any somewhat modern computer with a few simple tricks. With some setups, you don't need "tricks" at all.

Here are the hardware options I'm going to "officially" discuss in the book:

- Regular computers running Windows
- Apple computers running MacOS (Formerly called OSX)
- Regular computers running Linux
- Raspberry Pi running Linux (It's basically just a really scaled-down PC)
- Chromebooks
- Tablets (either Android or iOS)
- Smartphones (either Android or iOS)

The last three options, Chromebooks, tablets, and

smartphones can't natively run a command line or installed apps in a terminal. They will require you to use an SSH app to log into a remote server "in the cloud." I will describe this process first. Again, these three systems <u>must</u> do it this way, while the Windows, Mac, and Linux people have the added option of running command line apps locally.

Even so, I would recommend that everyone read the next section, and even if you are running a Mac or PC, you may find the Chromebook method is more appealing to you. Any system can SSH into a remote server, and if you don't want to install text apps on your local system, then this is a "will work for everyone" option.

Linux on Chromebook Note: I'm not going to cover the process here, but it is also completely possible to install Linux on a Chromebook. If this is something you want to explore, just install Linux and then follow along the rest of the book as if you were running a Linux PC. Here's a website to get you started: https://www.lifewire.com/install-linux-on-chromebook-4125253

Still, I am assuming you bought a Chromebook because you wanted the regular features of a Chromebook, not for Linux use, so the rest of the book assumes you are not going this route and plan to use the Chromebook in the "usual" way.

Smartphone Note: Most of what I suggest about tablets will also work without alteration on smartphones, either of the Android or Apple variety. That's not to say this is a good solution; the onscreen keyboards and tiny screens, even on larger phones, are going to make getting real work done in text a "visual challenge." You can do it, but I don't really recommend it for more than doing casual updates of files. Still, it *can* be done, and sometimes that's reason enough.

Tablet Note: The only special thing I can say pertaining to tablets is that external keyboards are a wonderful thing. A big portion of the benefit of going with the command line is the benefit gained from being able to use a keyboard for everything, and an on-screen keyboard is going to slow you down. You certainly can use the onscreen keyboard, and for portability reasons that's sometime desirable, but for long-term, sitting-at-a-desk work, I'd recommend getting a good Bluetooth keyboard.

GETTING TO A COMMAND LINE

The people who work on building graphical operating systems (Microsoft, Apple, and the Linux crew) have gone to great lengths to make it unnecessary to get into the command line very often. Some people have never even tried to find one. So in the (usually rare) cases when something must be done on a command line, some people find it nearly traumatic. It's not that bad. Really. Back in the 80s, this was all we had! Still, you've made it this far, so you're probably not too terrified at the idea. This chapter is where we figure out how to get access to the ~~Gateway to Hell~~ command line.

USING ANY DEVICE: REMOTE SERVERS
AND SSH

Smartphones, Tablets, and Chromebooks

These three systems aren't typical computers in the usual sense. All three platforms have a thousand times the processing power of the text-based computers of the 90's, but they can't run a command line in the usual way. So we'll have to get to a command line via a different tool— using SSH to log into a remote server.

This method allows you access to everything that's text-only-- there are still issues with playing music and videos through SSH, but if you're running a tablet or Chromebook, you already have the tools to do that, albeit not through text.

What Remote Server?

First of all, a remote server is a computer that runs Linux (in this situation) that isn't anywhere you have physical access to it. You connect to the other computer and log in through the Internet. Everything you do is done on the other, remote, computer, but it uses the screen and keyboard in front of you; the brains of the system is somewhere else.

This is taking the very old concept of client/server computing and running it as a modern "cloud" system; same thing, new terminology. If you're familiar with the way Chromebooks work (software doesn't run locally, but in the cloud), then this is the same essential idea. Your files are hosted elsewhere, and you access them through the Internet.

If you're technologically-oriented enough to find the idea of Going Text appealing, you may already have a server that you can log into. Many web hosting services offer SSH access. Perhaps your work or school has something you can use.

If you don't already have some kind of server, there are inexpensive commercial options available. I'm going to recommend one called Digital Ocean. For five dollars a month, you get SSH access to a machine running your choice of operating systems (I use Ubuntu Linux). A similar offering can be found from the competing company Linode, and there are certainly others out there available.

Digital Ocean offers a system with a single-CPU, 1 GB RAM, 25 GB SSD Hard Drive, and 1 Terabyte of data transfer for only five dollars a month. Those specs may look pretty low compared to buying a computer, but remember that we're going to mostly be dealing with text files through a terminal program, which are tiny and require very little space or Internet bandwidth. Additionally, five dollars a month may sound expensive compared to running, say, a Raspberry Pi, but considering they set up everything for you and manage the hardware, security, backups, maintenance, and the fact that you can access your files anywhere, then it's a bargain. If it turns out you need more space, or more speed, it's easily expandable. If this method doesn't appeal to you for some reason, then you can always set up a server yourself in your home and access it through the Chromebook, Tablet, or your Smartphone. Setting up your own Linux server is beyond the scope of this book, but it's not too hard if you want to give it a shot.

Sign up for the minimal account at Digital Ocean, then create a droplet running the latest version of Ubuntu. Next, add your user account, and you're ready to begin. All of this can be done from a web browser on any device, even your phone. Digital Ocean isn't the only way to get a server, so I don't want to spend too much space on how to set up the server. Digital Ocean offers the following tutorial on how get set up and ready to start:

```
https://www.digitalocean.com/community/tuto
rials/initial-server-setup-with-
ubuntu-16-04
```

Once you have a server ready to use, you need some way to connect to it. You will need an app called an SSH Client. SSH is the protocol that your local computer uses to connect with the remote one. It's something like the HTTP in the web browser, but for interactive text-based (mostly) interfaces. If you are an old-timer, you may remember something called *Telnet*. SSH is basically like Telnet, but with added security and encryption.

For Chromebooks that cannot run Android apps, or optionally for use on **any computer that has Chrome installed**, I would recommend a web app simply called **Secure Shell**, available at

```
https://chrome.google.com/webstore/detail/s
ecure-
```

```
shell/pnhechapfaindjhompbnflcldabbghjo?
utm_source=chrome-app-launcher
```

The screenshot below shows Secure Shell running on
Chrome. If you switched the browser into full-screen mode,
you wouldn't even see the bar at the top of the screen. It
works really well, and it's free.

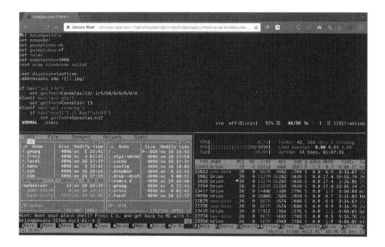

Secure Shell within Chrome Browser

For Android or iOS systems, I recommend an app called
Termius https://www.termius.com/. It's completely func-
tional in the free version, but has a few added bells and
whistles if you buy the Pro version (I use the free one, and
never saw a need for more). Termius works quite well on
tablets, but also allows smartphone use. Although I've not
tried it, I have also heard very good things about **Blink** for
iOS, found at http://www.blink.sh/ . The following screenshot shows Termius running as an Android app on a
Chromebook Pro:

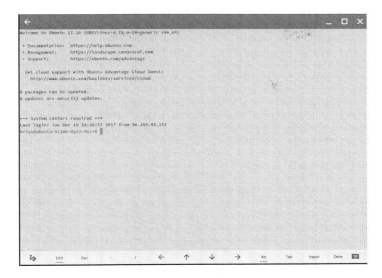

Termius for Android

There are many other possible (and excellent) apps on every platform, so look around and choose one with a price and features that you like; the only requirement is that it can do SSH and allows some way to use all the standard keyboard keys, for example 'ESC' if your usual device keyboard doesn't offer that already.

WINDOWS COMPUTERS

Option One: SSH

First, if you prefer, you can use the preceding chapter to setup and SSH into a remote server. You can use the **Secure Shell** Chrome app, just as with a Chromebook. Another option is to use the SSH app called **PuTTY**. PuTTY is a SSH terminal app similar to Termius, described in the previous section. To use this method, just install PuTTY or Secure Shell and use them to connect to your Digital Ocean or other remote server.

Option Two: Powershell and Command Line

Here it gets tricky. Windows has been trying to get away from the command line since Windows 95 tried to replace DOS back in the mid-90s. Microsoft really didn't want you to use the command line, but it never really made it impossible.

That said, most apps went with a standard Windows GUI interface and the command line languished. Still, a large number of open-sourced Linux apps have been modified and adapted to work from the Windows command line. VIM, Emacs, and a few other major players can be used locally from the regular Windows command line. On the other hand, this isn't the best way to go with the command line.

Option Three: Windows Subsystem for Linux

This is the way I'm going to recommend that you do the command line apps in Windows. This is a relatively recent addition to Windows, and requires Windows 10. If you aren't familiar with the Windows Subsystem for Linux, Microsoft has a nice overview at:

https://blogs.msdn.microsoft.com/wsl/2016/04/22/windows-subsystem-for-linux-overview/
And they also have an excellent tutorial on how to install it at https://docs.microsoft.com/en-us/windows/wsl/install-win10

Installing Ubuntu on Windows

This allows you to run many, if not most of the major text-only apps created for Linux from within a command line prompt on Windows. You start Windows normally, launch the Linux Subsystem from a menu like any other app, and then you have a Linux command line. When we get to the app section, you will download apps using the same process (*apt-get*) as you would if this were a normal Linux system.

At some point, you will have to decide which Linux "Distribution" you want to install. For now, I'll suggest going with **Ubuntu** unless you have some specific reason for choosing something else. The section later in this chapter discussing Linux will explain why I chose that one.

Linux for Windows Subsystem

MAC COMPUTERS

Just as with Windows, if you prefer to use Chrome and Secure Shell to SSH into a remote server, that's always an option. There are some native MacOS apps that you can use as well:

Terminal

The **Terminal** app is in the Applications->Utilities folder and is installed by default on all Macs. You can customize it somewhat with fonts and colors, but it's pretty barebones otherwise.

Mac Terminal

iTerm2

This is a free and open-source replacement for the Apple Terminal app, and it adds many nice features, including split panes, hotkeys, search, colors, triggers, and a lot more. Check out the app and the full feature list at https://iterm2.com/features.html

iTerm 2 for Apple

Apple Package Manager Note:

The usual Linux methods of installing software won't work. Instead of "apt-get install" you need to use "Homebrew" or something similar— see https://brew.sh/. The installation instructions on that page are very easy, and will install what is called a "package manager" for MacOS. This package manager will then allow you to easily install command line tools like this:

```
brew install packagename
```

Homebrewing Software

LINUX COMPUTERS

There's no special "App" you need to install to get to a command line from within Linux. All versions of Linux have some variation of a command line terminal app.

Distributions/Distros

A *Distribution* can be looked at as a kind of "brand" of Linux. Any group can create their own selection of Linux apps and utilities and release it as a "distribution." Some distributions focus on ease of installation, some focus on security, some focus on attractive presentations, and some focus on minimalism-- There are hundreds of distributions available. Some of the most popular ones are Ubuntu, Fedora, Arch, Mint, and Gentoo. You'll find people who advocate one or the other, often quite zealously, but as far as the availability of text-based tools are concerned, there isn't much difference between them. Find one that installs and works well on your system, and it will be fine for our purposes.

Why Ubuntu?

If you already have a favorite Linux distribution, feel free to use it; as I just pointed out, it doesn't make much difference with text-based apps. If you don't know much about Linux, or are undecided, I am going to suggest Ubuntu. Why? Because it installs without issue on every computer I have attempted it on, the instructions are straightforward, and it's so popular that it's in constant development-- it's not going to go away anytime soon. Also, if you need assistance, it's one of the most heavily-used distributions, so it's not hard to find someone who can help you.

Package Managers

The only major difference between Linux distributions that you need to be aware of initially is that they all use different "package managers" or methods of installing new software.

To install software with Ubuntu, you type the following:

```
sudo apt-get install packagename
```

Where packagename is the name of the program you want to install. Other distributions do it differently. For example, Fedora Linux uses:

```
sudo rpm —ivh packagename.rpm
```

And Arch Linux uses:

```
sudo pacman -S packagename
```

All three of these do the same thing; they install the

program called "packagename." In my instructions that follow, I'll be using the Ubuntu apt-get method, because that's what I use. If you aren't using Ubuntu, you will need to modify the commands accordingly.

MacOS Note: Although MacOS isn't a Linux distribution, the process to install command line software is similar. To make it a little more complex, Mac doesn't offer apt-get or any kind of built-in package manager. You'll need to install one first: "Homebrew" is a good one: https://brew.sh/ The installation instructions on that page are very easy, and will install the "Homebrew package manager" for MacOS. This package manager will then allow you to easily install command line tools. To compare with the examples above, you would type:

```
brew install packagename
```

Similar to what you would type within Linux.

OPTIONS SUMMARY

So, by this time, I am going to assume you have some way to get to a command line via one of the following:

- On a Mac Using Terminal or iTerm2 (and you have Homebrew installed)
- On Windows 10 using Linux Subsystem for Windows
- On any PC using Linux
- On Windows using PuTTY to SSH to a remote server
- On any device using a Chrome browser and Secure Shell to SSH to a remote server
- A smartphone or tablet using some kind of SSH App to connect to a remote server

So in effect, we'll only be talking about Linux commands from here on out, as Linux command line tools work on ALL the above hardware choices and setups.

USING THE COMMAND LINE: THE TOOLS

You've got a window or screen full of big empty blankness in front of you. What next? Now it's time to set up the tools we'll need to get work done. This section covers a few general-purpose power tools that make getting around in the command line easier.

TMUX

With a GUI like Windows or MacOS, when you want to run more than one app at a time, you simply run each app in its own little window. With text-mode terminal apps, you only have one screen, so you need to split that screen up into sections and run one app in each section.

Tmux in use

Tmux is what is known as a "terminal multiplexer." That's a fancy way of saying it splits your terminal window into smaller panes that each can run a separate program. The image above shows a single terminal window running two apps: Vim and a directory listing. The image on the cover of this book shows four apps running in a single terminal window. This is all done through Tmux. You can install Tmux easily by typing the following command into the terminal:

```
sudo apt-get install tmux
```

or on a Mac (after you've installed Homebrew as previously discussed), try:

```
brew install tmux
```

Installing Tmux Software through Homebrew

The latest version of Tmux will download and install, and automatically also install any other libraries or files that the app needs to run. Once it's installed, just type

```
tmux
```

at the command line, and you're up and running. It doesn't look like much; probably all you will notice is a colored bar at the bottom of the window. This is typical of command-line apps; they often don't have fancy menus. You control Tmux by pressing the Tmux "command key," which by default is ***CTRL-B***. To make something happen, you press CTRL-B and some other key depending on what you want to do. For example, to split the screen vertically, as in the picture above, press CTRL-B, then press %. Note that to get to %, you also have to hold down the SHIFT key, so that really works out to be CTRL-B then SHIFT-5 (to get % on a US keyboard).

Here is a quick list of the most commonly used Tmux commands. You can split the screen into multiple PANES, and/or you can have multiple WINDOWS, which are whole screens.

Action	Key Combination (^ means CTRL)
Split Window Vertically	^b %
Split Window Horizontally	^b "
New Window	^b c
Close window	^d OR ^b x
Kill window	^b &
Next window	^b n
Previous window	^b p
Rename window	^b ,
List all windows	^b w
Move to window number	^b [number]
Next pane	^b o
Previous pane	^b ;
Show pane numbers	^b q
Move pane left	^b {
Move pane right	^b }
Swap pane locations	^b ^o
Resize pane down	^b ^j
Resize pane up	^b ^k
Resize pane left	^b ^h
Resize pane right	^b ^l

Tmux Commands

That *looks* like a lot to remember, but you'll catch on to them quickly enough with use. In the beginning, all you need to remember is CONTROL-B then either % or " to split the window either vertically or horizontally, then use CONTROL-B and the arrow keys to navigate between the panes.

It good to get into the habit of opening the terminal app of your choice, then loading Tmux immediately before anything else. That way if you find yourself needing another app, you can just pop open another window and have it right there.

TERMINATOR

Tmux runs in a general terminal window and splits up what you see in different ways. Terminator replaces the terminal app itself, and runs multiple resizable terminal panels in one window.

This one isn't a text-based app exactly, it's a replacement for the Linux terminal itself. If you aren't running a straight-forward Linux system, or you'd prefer to stick with the more commonly used Tmux method of splitting screens, you can skip this one. To install (again, this one is Linux only):

```
sudo apt-get install terminator
```

A Whole Bunch of Terminator Panes

Help can be found at **Terminator: The Robot Future of Terminals**

https://gnometerminator.blogspot.in/p/introduction.html

RANGER AND MIDNIGHT COMMANDER

Ranger and Midnight Commander can be installed by

```
sudo apt-get ranger
or
sudo apt-get mc
```

Both Midnight Commander and Ranger are File Managers. They allow you to easily navigate your computer's folder hierarchy and copy, move, rename, and delete files, as well as look at previews of the file contents.

It's completely possible to ignore these two and simply copy files with Unix commands like *cp, mv, rm, ls*, and so forth, and sometimes it *is* faster to simply type out your commands. It'd definitely be smart to learn all the Unix file-manipulation commands so you *can* do things quickly. If you like purely working at a command-line shell, like this, one, you are always free to do so:

File Listing on the Plain Command Line

Sometimes, on the other hand, you want to do things with batches of files or more visually browse and navigate your files. Both Midnight Commander and Ranger are good in their own ways, but it's probably most efficient to pick one or the other and get really good with it.

Ranger has a more "open" feel to it, with two levels of directory in the leftmost two panes, and a file preview in the third pane. Movement is fast and highly visual, but there aren't any controls or menus on screen-- it's *all* done through memorized keyboard commands.

File Listing with Ranger

Midnight Commander, on the other hand, offers a permanent two-column view. This is nice for copying files or comparing folders. There are also menus at the top of the screen, which are easily navigable by either the keyboard or (gasp!) the mouse.

File Listing with Midnight Commanders

Which one you use is entirely up to you. I generally do most file-moving commands things right on the command line. If I want to quickly move to a song or load a text file, I'll zoom quickly to it in Ranger. When I'm doing something with deeply-nested paths, or on the occasion where I don't know where something is, I'll use Midnight Commander.

USING THE COMMAND LINE - THE APPS

And now that you can get to a command line and move things around in there, it's time to get some real work done. I'll show you a few examples of the most common and popular commands to do most tasks, but keep in mind that people have been doing these tasks using similar tools for decades; there are probably dozens of solutions for each task available, and people are still comping up with new ways of doing the same things, so after you've looked at my suggestions, do a little Internet research and see if there's some way that fits *your* workflows better.

WRITING TOOLS

Probably the main task for most people (other than maybe browsing the web and email) is writing. Whether it's simple notes, emails, or full-length books, there are some great text-only tools to do the job. Unlike, say, Microsoft Word or Apple Pages, you can't just highlight a word and make it bold or italic in a terminal window. You usually will need to use some kind of a **markup language** such as Markdown or LaTeX (see the "Advanced Topics" section). Like almost everything else involved with switching to text, it's *more* difficult in the beginning, but far more efficient and speedy once you know how it works.

Nano

Nano usually comes pre-installed on most Linux systems. It's a really, *really* basic text editor. It's actually almost *too* basic for most useful tasks– your customization options are very limited. That said, it's probably on your system already, and it's fine for quickly reading or making a fast change to a file. Not only that, but all the functions are easily discoverable via the two-line menu on the bottom of the screen. It's not the "Editor of a lifetime," but it *may* be all you need.

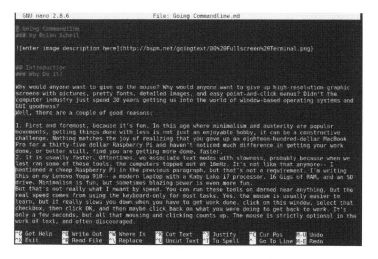

Nano Text Editor

Vim

```
sudo apt-get install vim
```

Vim and Emacs were designed to be text editors for coders, and if you're a programmer, either of these would be outstanding choices for you to master. Either one can be adapted for darned near anything, as every single feature has customization options.

Vim, at least in my opinion, is a bit harder to learn at first, but well worth it once you get past the learning curve. It's a *modal* editor, meaning that you move around and navigate in one mode, type text in another mode, and visually select things in a third mode. It's a little unusual coming from Microsoft Word, but there's a lot of power there once you learn how the thing works.

Vim Text Editor

Emacs

```
sudo apt-get install emacs
```

Then there's Emacs. There are people who type stuff, check their email, add appointments to their calendars, change their to-do lists, and browse the web... All without leaving Emacs. It's easier to get started with than Vim, but the more you use it, the deeper the bottomless pit of Emacs becomes. Someone working at the "expert level" of Emacs could probably do everything we talk about in this book... *without leaving Emacs.* There are people who jokingly call Emacs an operating system in itself, it's almost not a joke.

With both Emacs and Vim, nearly any aspect of the

editor can be customized and made to work in many different ways. There are also add-ins, themes, and extensions that allow you to do things you'd never imagine you could in a text editor. It's always been a tough call deciding between the two.

Emacs Text Editor

Wordgrinder

```
sudo apt-get install wordgrinder
```

All three of the proceeding editors were originally designed with programming/coding in mind. Wordgrinder comes at writing from a different perspective. It's more of a word-processor designed for writers. It has easy-to-use menus, the arrow keys work like you'd expect, and there are very few surprises here. You can make words bold or italic easily right in the text, and you don't need to learn Markdown or special coding.

It's not very customizable; it pretty much works as it comes. There aren't any plug-ins or fancy themes. It's reliable, simple to use, and it simply works.

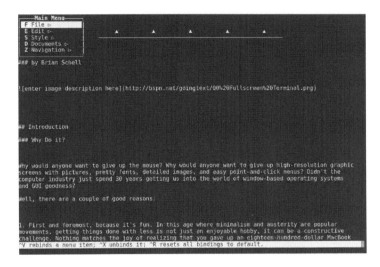

Wordgrinder Word Processor

My recommendation is to look at both Nano and Wordgrinder first. Nano is great for quick and dirty text editing, while Wordgrinder can handle most writing tasks. If you decide you really want to become a "Text Master," give Vim and/or Emacs a shot.

EMAIL

Probably the primary business use of most computers today, email is a crucial tool. However, due to the prevalence of hackers and spammers, security with email is a major concern. That makes setting up an email client one of the most challenging tasks we're going to run into.

Sendmail

This one is generally a little iffy. Sendmail is a notoriously difficult app to set up, and due to the possibility of being hacked or abused, it's best left to experts. Your system *might* have it already set up and configured, so it's worth giving it a try. Just type a message into a text file, save it, and type something similar to the following:

```
sendmail user@example.com < message.txt
```

Another option would be to try:

```
sendmail -t user@example.com
```

...and then type your message below that. Hit CTRL-D to send the message or CTRL-C to abort. This will either work or it won't. Again, I recommend that if this doesn't "just work" out of the box for you, that you move on to other options.

Mutt

```
sudo apt-get install mutt
```

Mutt (and Alpine) are much more complete email clients. You get a full interface to search, sort, read, and reply to your emails, and it's easy to deal with multiple folders and message attachments. Which you choose depends on what you need and which one you find more attractive and usable. They both do pretty much the same things.

One major disadvantage that I have found with Mutt is that it stores your passwords in the configuration files in plain text. If anyone got into your system, they could easily look at your email passwords and cause you a world of trouble. You *can* use Mutt and not have it store the passwords, but then you will need to re-enter your email password every time you load Mutt, which is inconvenient, to say the least.

Mutt Email Client

Alpine

```
sudo apt-get install alpine
```

Alpine doesn't have the same ease of customization that Mutt has, but it does have the ability to store encrypted passwords on the server. If you have a remote system (i.e. you SSH into it) and you don't want to be bothered typing your email password every time, this is the better option.

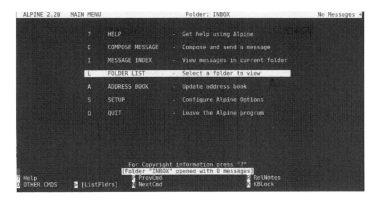

Alpine Email Client

OTHER "OFFICE" APPS

Writing and Email are a big deal for most of us, but a great deal of useful work also involves numbers and presentations. In the GUI world, there is Microsoft Excel and Powerpoint, or even LibreOffice. Those don't apply on the command line, so we need to find something similar.

SC and SC-IM

SC is short for Screen Calculator, otherwise known as a spreadsheet for text mode. It does all the basic stuff that spreadsheets like Excel do, but does it all through the keyboard and text screen. It wants to save all its files in CSV (Comma-separated values) but it can read in Excel files. It allows right and left text alignment, cut and paste, and various decimal formatting options as well as a huge number of calculation and math functions. It's not as pretty as a GUI spreadsheet, but the power is all there. The original SC program was created around 13 years ago; the SC-IM fork is still being developed and maintained.

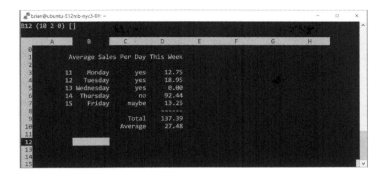

SC Spreadsheet Calculator

Presentations

Out in the world of Windows and Mac, PowerPoint, Keynote, Present, or even Google Slides are available for presentations. Slideshow presentations *scream* for graphics, so a text-based presentation may not be the best way to go most of the time. Still, sometimes you want to do something just to show that you *can* do a thing, so here are your presentation options: Beamer, Vimdeck, and MDP.

Beamer isn't an *app* per se, it's an extension of LaTeX (See the section on Advanced Topics) that allows you to create a file using a text editor and then output it as a PDF that can be shown on a projector, printed out, or emailed to recipients. It allows colored text, graphics, diagrams, and basically any kind of media that is supported by LaTeX. It doesn't do any kind of animation (it outputs in PDF after all), but any static imagery can be used.

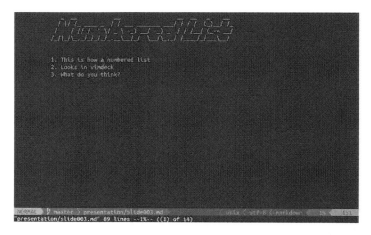

Vimdeck Presentation

Vimdeck is a tool that allows you to write a file using markdown (See the section on Advanced Topics) and compile it into a presentation that can be viewed using Vim. You don't have to use Vim to create the file, but the final presentation is optimized for use within Vim.

MDP is actually an app that runs a presentation in text. Beamer and Vimdeck were tools to create presentation files, while MDP takes markdown text and does the actual presentation, with lots of nice options including color, citations, headers, nested lists, and lots of other text-based (still no graphics) elements.

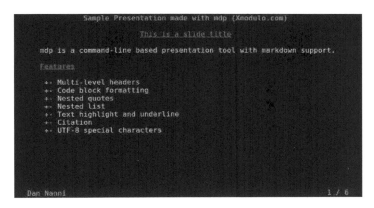

MDP Presentation

NOTES APPS

Terminal Velocity

Terminal Velocity is a fairly recent app inspired by the OSX app called Notational Velocity. To create a new note, type a title for the note and hit enter. The note will be opened in your text editor. As you type the title, the list of notes filters to show notes that match what you've typed, giving you a chance to open a related note instead of making a new one. This means that you use the same line to type a new note as you do to search for an existing one; which makes the whole process of searching and creating very fast. I use this one in conjunction with Dropbox to keep my notes with me on all my devices.

Emacs Org Mode

We've already discussed Emacs in the Writing Apps section, but it deserves another mention here. "Org mode" is a special mode that Emacs offers that allows you to type in text that is viewed as a sort of outline. You write files in

Markdown, but you can also use the TAB key to quickly collapse or expand outline trees, move whole sections up and down, and quickly create things like to-do lists, outlines, and notes of all kinds. If you already have some familiarity with Emacs, it's easy to get started using Org mode, but there is so much you can do with it the options can get extensive.

```
#+TITLE: Example .org file
#+AUTHOR: Bastien
#+DATE: 2012-09-08 sam.

* Make a new website for orgmode.org

** TODO Make screenshots
   SCHEDULED: <2012-09-07 ven.>

** NEXT [#A] Add them to the website
   SCHEDULED: <2012-09-08 sam.>

** NEXT Publish the new website
   DEADLINE: <2012-09-09 dim.>

* Plain-text tables and spreadsheet...
* Working with source code █
-:--  website.org   Top L27   (0) ((Org +S P.1)) sam. sept.  @ 06:15 0.90
[No changes need to be saved]
```

Emacs ORG mode file

SECURITY

One thing you don't generally have to worry about when using Linux is viruses. Due to the way everything is split up and restricted by usernames and permissions, it's much harder to catch a virus than on, say, a Windows machine. That does not, however, mean you don't still have to be concerned about security. One major area of concern worth looking at is password security.

Pass is a password management system. It can keep track of a database of thousands of web sites and passwords, and is especially useful in creating secure passwords. You can request a new password, specifying the number of symbols, and it generates what you need, completely randomly and copies it to the clipboard.

This kind of app is tremendously helpful. I've gone from weak passwords such as

```
USER: brianschell
PASSWORD: PENCIL  (or the cat's name or something)
to
USER: brianschell
```

```
PASSWORD: zagw@JPTfVquVkQjvAetx2ZiA
```

Obviously, a password like that is hard, if not impossible, to remember. Or type for that matter; fortunately, Pass will copy the password into the clipboard for you. You can find the full documentation for Pass at

https://www.passwordstore.org

WEB BROWSERS

Wait– browsing the web in text mode? Yes you can!

The following three browsers have all been around for decades, and all three have the ability to deal with mostly-text websites. Some allow for image viewing through external viewers, while some allow in-line image viewing with plug-ins. None are as robust or pretty as modern GUI browsers, but they often can get the job done.

There *are* benefits to using text-mode browsers. First, they are blazing fast compared to graphical browsers– they don't run the embedded Javascript codes, and they don't download all those images (including the invisible tracking images). Since all they do is download the text, they're fast even on a slow system. Also, because they're text-only, they allow easy integration with text-to-speech software and work very well for the visually impaired.

Lynx

This is the oldest of the browsers, as it was first begun as a project in 1992. Due to this longevity, it's quite stable and safe. It doesn't work with sites requiring Javascript, but does handle sites with cookies.

Lynx Browser

W3M

W3M is also quite old, begun in 1995. It has support for tables, frames, SSL connections, color, and inline images on suitable terminals. Generally, it renders pages in a form as true to their original layout as possible. W3M is one of the more actively-maintained browsers, and has many extensions and plugins, so this may be the best choice if you need to do a lot of text-based web use.

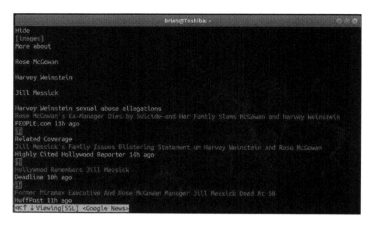

W3M Browser

ELinks

This is the most "modern-looking" of the three. It has a color display, and when you press the ESC key, navigation menus appear that make the whole thing easier to figure out. It supports the mouse, tabs, cookies, and more.

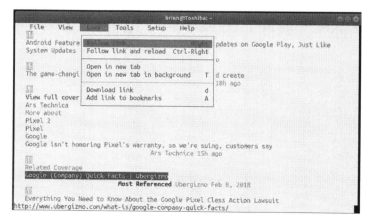

Elinks Browser

COMMUNICATIONS

IRC: WeeChat and IRSSI

One of the most popular things to do back when the Internet started becoming available to everyone was to hang out in IRC Chat rooms. Before Facebook, before Google+, even back before MySpace, there was IRC (Internet Relay Chat). Believe it or not, IRC is still very popular and still going strong, especially among the tech community. There are numerous ways to get on IRC, even through the command line. Both of the apps presented here, WeeChat and IRSSI, are actively developed and going strong.

Both offer scripting, plug-ins, themes, filters, help screens, and everything else you need to get started.

WeeChat IRC Client

VOIP

As far as I know, there is no command line replacement for Skype, Facetime, or other VOIP software. There is an "experimental" project called Twinkle that exists, but is reported to be crash-prone and unreliable. If this is something you badly need, you might want to take a look. https://github.com/LubosD/twinkle.

SOCIAL MEDIA

Twitter

You wouldn't think Twitter clients would be all that hard to come by, but there's only one that I could really recommend: **Rainbow Stream**. It's easy to install and configure, and it allows you post, narrow the stream into List view, and most anything else you would want to do with Twitter.

```
sudo pip install rainbowstream
```

Installation instructions can be found at http://rainbowstream.readthedocs.io/en/latest/

Facebook

There's not a "regular" Facebook client for the command line, but you can use their site through any of the text-based web browsers. There is, however, a command-line client for Facebook *Messenger*.

```
sudo apt-get install npm
sudo npm install -g fb-messenger-cli
```

GRAPHICS, ART, AND PHOTOS

Asciiview

For years, our cameras have been advertising more and
more megapixels. Sometimes, once in a while, it's more fun
to go the other way around and look for the lowest resolu-
tions possible. One of those cases would be when you need
to display a photograph or graphic image on a text-only
terminal. One way to get this done is to use Asciiview.

```
sudo apt-get aview
aview myphoto.bpm
```

The Author's Photo in Asciiview

Figlet

Figlet is just a little command line tool to take a line of text and make a "Banner" from it.

```
sudo apt-get install figlet
```

and then:

```
figlet Brian
```

ImageMagick

Both the above Ascii apps are little more than toys. Sometimes you need to actually get work done, and for that, there's ImageMagick.

```
sudo apt-get install imagemagick
https://www.imagemagick.org/script/command-
line-processing.php
```

There are tools to create, edit, compose, or convert bitmap images. It can read and write images in a variety of formats (over 200) including PNG, JPEG, GIF, HEIC, TIFF, DPX, EXR, WebP, Postscript, PDF, and SVG. Use ImageMagick to resize, flip, mirror, rotate, distort, shear and transform images, adjust image colors, apply various special effects, or draw text, lines, polygons, ellipses and Bézier curves.

The ImageMagick command-line tools can be as simple as this, converting from one format to another:

```
magick image.jpg image.png
```

Or it can be complex with a plethora of options, as in the following:

```
magick label.gif +matte ( +clone -shade
110x90 -normalize -negate +clone -compose
Plus -composite ) ( -clone 0 -shade 110x50
-normalize -channel BG -fx 0 +channel -
matte ) -delete 0 +swap -compose Multiply -
composite button.gif");
```

AUDIO AND VIDEO

Music Players

The computer can get pretty boring at times with just text on the screen. Fortunately, you don't have to sit there and work in silence. Any computer with sound capability can play excellent music, and the command line has numerous excellent (and very customizable) music players. My two favorites are MOC and CMUS.

Both work better if you have your music library organized in artist directories. At one point, I had all my music in Apple iTunes, so I just downloaded all the songs, copied the giant "Music" folder to its own directory, and pointed the music players at them-- the default organization leftover from iTunes worked without any modification. I'm not saying you *need* iTunes to organize your music, but a lot of people already have that somewhere, and if you do, it's one easy way to go.

MOC (Music On Console)

I like this one especially when I am working with a playlist. It has two columns, and the default layout looks a lot like **Midnight Commander.** You can see your music files on the left pane, and the playlist you are working with on the right pane. Select a file, "add" it to the list, and you can visually see what you're doing. It's theme-able, has an equalizer built in, the keys can be remapped to your preferences, and even has support for Internet streams. It's got a convenient help screen, just hit "H", and all the commands pop up for you.

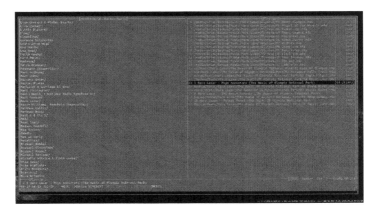

MOC (Music on Console)

CMUS (C Music Player)

While MOC is great for working with playlists, I like CMUS better for just browsing and playing songs on a whim; the navigation feels nicer to me. While MOC has a navigation system reminiscent of Midnight Commander, CMUS looks and feels more like **Ranger.** Your choice of music player may be closely related to which file browsing system you prefer.

It supports most music formats from the default install: Ogg Vorbis, MP3, FLAC, Opus, Musepack, WavPack, WAV, AAC, MP4, audio CD, and everything supported by ffmpeg (WMA, APE, MKA, TTA, SHN, ...) and libmodplug.

Like MOC, CMUS has re-mappable keys, theming, and color customizing. This one, however, also allows for music streaming from online radio stations if you can find the url for the stream, i.e. http://beirutnights.com/live.m3u

C MUSic Player

MPC/MPD (Music Play Daemon/Controller)

Both of the previous entries, MOC and CMUS, were full-screen apps that relied heavily on visually navigating files and directories. Both interfaces were inspired by file management systems, and both are at least somewhat inter-active with their controls.

An alternative is the Music Play Daemon, or MPD. It is a flexible, powerful, server-side application for playing music.

Through plugins and libraries it can play a variety of sound files while being controlled by its network protocol. Since it's a daemon, it just runs silently in the background and waits for commands from an external client program.

MPC is the parallel Client App. It connects to MPD and controls it according to commands and arguments passed to it. If no arguments are passed, current status is given. It's strictly a command-line tool, with no visuals whatsoever.

There are, however, a number of *other* clients that work with the MPD server. Some are graphical, some are for the web, while others are for use on the console. It's a bit harder to set up, but it's *very* flexible and powerful.

MPD Daemon Homepage https://www.musicpd.org/
MPD Clients https://www.musicpd.org/clients/

Movie Viewers

Movies are obviously visual. There are going to be some text-only console setups that cannot play movies, as graphics are simply a must for video. You cannot play movies through a strict console terminal. That said, many people run command-line programs from within some kind of graphical interface, such as Windows, MacOS, or XOrg. These systems can play videos, and sometimes you'll want to start and control playback through the command line.

MPlayer is a movie player which runs on many systems. It plays most MPEG/VOB, AVI, Ogg/OGM, VIVO, ASF, WMA, WMV, QT, MOV, MP4, RealMedia, Matroska, NUT, NuppelVideo, FLI, YUV4MPEG, FILM, RoQ, PVA files, supported by many native, XAnim, and Win32 DLL codecs. You can watch VideoCD, SVCD, DVD, 3ivx, DivX 3/4/5, WMV and even H.264 movies.

Another great feature of MPlayer is the wide range of supported output drivers. It works with Xii, Xv, DGA, OpenGL, SVGAlib, fbdev, AAlib, DirectFB, but you can use GGI, SDL (and this way all their drivers), VESA (on every VESA compatible card, even without Xii) and some low level card-specific drivers. Most of them support software or hardware scaling, so you can enjoy movies in full screen or in a window.

Even with all this, you still may not be able to watch videos on your hardware, but it's good to know you have the ability if you need it.

MPlayer status on the left, MPlayer movie on the right

NEWS AND WEATHER

News

News is mostly text, so it's not a huge leap to see that there would be a number of ways to get the news on the command line. Here are two great ways to get started:

Instantnews retrieves all news headlines from the News API, then displays what you want to see in text. There are dozens of professional news sources, and you can choose from one or any combination of them to display on your screen. It requires you to sign up for a free API key. The instructions and links are found at:

```
https://github.com/shivam043/instantnews
```

A slightly more "fun" news program that works similarly is **Haxor-News.** Haxor-news brings hacker and nerd news to the terminal, allowing you to view and filter the following without leaving your command line:

- Posts
- Post Comments
- Post-Linked Web Content
- Monthly Hiring and Freelancers Posts
- User Info
- Onion Posts

Install and run it as follows:

```
pip install haxor-news
haxor-news
```

Once you are in, you type various commands starting with "hn" such as "hn top" to show the top stories right now. Here is an example of the output:

Haxor News Top Stories

Once you find a story that you want to read, type "hn view #" to view that particular story. Here's what I get after entering "hn view 8".

News article about deceased film director

... and then hit "q" to go back to the article list and choose more. The full list of commands and help is found at https://github.com/donnemartin/haxor-news#installation

NewsBeuter/Newsboat are two names for the same program. Newsbeuter is an RSS reader. Many websites, including most news sources, offer an RSS feed containing their stories.

```
sudo apt-get install newsbeuter
```

then run the command "newsbeuter" to run it. On some systems, the command "newsboat" is used. Try one, and if it doesn't work, give the other a shot. Various commands will be displayed that show how to set it up. Once you have a collection of RSS feed installed in it, you will see something like this:

Newsbeuter/Newsboat List of Feeds

Of course, all the documentation is at

```
https://newsbeuter.org/index.html
```

Weather

There are a great many utilities for getting weather information from the command line, so here are a few fun apps:

For the lucky people who live in a supported city, you can simply type

```
finger city@graph.no
```

at the command line, substituting your city name for "city" in the command:

Getting the weather for New York City

Alternately, you can simply type

```
curl wttr.in/your_location
```

at the command line, substituting your city name for "your_location" in the command:

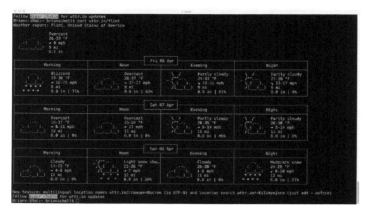

Getting the weather for Flint, MI

Another neat one, **ansiweather**, displays all your weather data on a single line.

```
sudo apt-get ansiweather
ansiweather -l Flint -u imperial -f 3
-s true
```

The example above looks up the weather for Flint and reports it for three days, in Imperial units (i.e. not metric) along with weather symbols.

AnsiWeather for Flint, MI

The full documentation for the command-line options can be found at https://github.com/fcambus/ansiweather

BOOKS, COMICS, AND READING

EPUB Documents

Generally, reading from the command line is done through a text editor such as Vim or Emacs, or even Nano. Still, more and more books are being made available in ebook formats. The only EPUB reader that I am aware of for the command line is at https://github.com/rupa/epub. Once installed, just type:

```
epub FILENAME.epub
```

...and the ebook (in EPUB format) will display on the screen. The instructions are on that page and are very easy to learn.

Non-EPUB formats:

Other ebook formats, such as .mobi, .azw and .prc will need to be converted to .epub or text format before use. The most common way to do this from within a graphical user interface is with the app Calibre. Since we're talking about command line tools here, most of Calibre's features won't be available, but Calibre DOES come with several powerful command line tools. If you are working on a GUI system (Windows, Mac, or Linux Desktop), you can install Calibre from https://calibre-ebook.com or the App Store of your choice.

Once you have Calibre installed, you can use its graphic interface if you choose, but if you want to do it all from the command line, check out the command-line tools installed alongside of Calibre.

Documented commands:

- calibre
- calibre-customize
- calibre-debug
- calibre-server
- calibre-smtp
- calibredb
- ebook-convert
- ebook-edit
- ebook-meta
- ebook-polish
- ebook-viewer
- fetch-ebook-metadata
- lrf2lrs
- lrfviewer
- lrs2lrf
- web2disk

The list and associated instructions can be found at:

https://manual.calibre-ebook.com/generated/en/cli-index.html. Probably the most useful one is ebook-convert. If you have a file in .mobi format, and you want to change it .epub format, just type:

```
ebook-convert myfile.mobi myfile.epub -h
```

It's really fast. Then you can just use the Epub reader to read the file.

TASK MANAGEMENT

There are many command line tools for calendaring, scheduling, and task management. Here are my favorites:

From way back in the early days of the original Unix systems, there is the ancient **cal** command. It displays a monthly calendar with today's date highlighted. I can't begin to tell how many times I've used this over the years. Other than displaying the month, it doesn't DO anything, but it's still incredibly convenient.

Calcurse

```
sudo apt-get install calcurse
calcurse
```

Calcurse is a text-based calendar, scheduler, and to-do manager for the command line. It has commands listed along the bottom two lines, much like the Nano editor, and additional commands can be had by hitting the 'o' key. It allows customizations of colors, the layout of the three main sections, and a few other things. If you aren't worried about syncing between your computer and other devices, this is probably the nicest way to go.

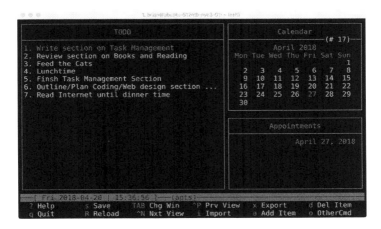

Calcurse

Todo.txt

If you are concerned about syncing your appointments and tasks between devices, this process is more complex, but allows for use on any device. The concept is simple: make a text file containing your to-do lists and appointments, then use a file-syncing system like Dropbox to make that file available to your computer, phone, tablet, and whatever other devices you use. It's easy to set this system up, it's reliable, and it's surprisingly flexible. If what I've just described is something that appeals to you, then by all means go for it right now and design your own methodology and system. Put a todo.txt file in your Dropbox on your phone and set your computer to access that file. You're all set!

On the other hand, some people have to get carried away. There's a whole online community that has built up around this idea, and they've come up with what they believe is a "standard" for todo.txt files. The home page for the organizations is at http://todotxt.org and the specific "rules" they have set up are at:

https://github.com/todotxt/todo.txt

I have also included their rules in the "Advanced Topics" section of the book. You might ask "Why use such a complicated set of rules for simply managing a todo list in a text file?" The answer is that if you use their standardized format, then you can take advantage of the various apps that have been created to support the format. There is **Todo.txt-cli** at https://github.com/todotxt/todo.txt-cli/releases as well as other apps that do the same thing. This idea especially appeals when you realize there are phone apps that work with these files as well. My favorite for the iPhone is **SwiftoDo**, found at http://swiftodoapp.com/. Text files and command lines are great on a full-sized computer, but on a little phone, specialized apps really are easier to use than trying to edit a text file.

SwiftoDo for iPhone

CODING/PROGRAMMING/WEB DESIGN

The options and availability of programming and coding tools are nearly unlimited. Almost every computer language compiler is available as a command line tool, and, under the surface , even most GUI programming tools simply run a command line tool in the background. The best way to get into coding is to choose a text editor program such as Vim, Emacs, or something of that sort and then start looking at the various syntax tools and programming-specific plugins. All the major text editors are used heavily by developers, mostly due to their customizability, plugin capability, and speed. Which editor you choose is largely a matter of taste and how much effort you want to put into learning it; it's completely possible to use nothing more than Nano to type in code and then compile it on the command line using the language of your choice, but most coders are going to want something more and will quickly advance into Emacs or Vim (although there are other choices out there that are excellent as well). There's no way I can even begin to scratch the surface of how to use these advanced editors in the development world, so I won't. Just keep in mind that coding in text mode is just as capable, if not more, as working in a GUI environment.

One coding tool that has exploded in the past few years is **Git.** Git is a free and open source distributed *version control system* designed to handle everything from small to very large projects with speed and efficiency. Git is easy to learn and has a tiny footprint with lightning-fast performance. It ties in with Github.com, the online repository and home of most of today's open source projects. The command line version of Git is available at https://git-scm.com and can be installed as either a command line version or GUI tool. Once you make some changes to a source file (whatever kind, from C++ to HTML to Prose Text), you commit changes to a repository, and then if you decide to branch off or restore from a previous version at a later time, you can. It's tremendously useful for keeping multiple versions of files, collaboration, and of course, bug fixes.

WEB APPS AND SERVICES

Installing command line software isn't the only option to get things done anymore. There are also countless web-applications available over the Internet for free or for a subscription fee. Some people survive just fine using nothing but a Chromebook as their primary computer, and, until recently, they used *nothing but* web applications... and we're looking at them in this book as almost an afterthought. Many advanced web pages depend heavily on scripting languages that do not work well (or at all) from a text-based browser, but some do.

There are command line tools to access to access many web-based services. **Todoist** is one very popular To-do list manager that works great on most mobile devices, and there is at least one good command line interface for it. The **Todo.txt** system is another system that works between mobile/GUI and Text. Google Drive (via the **Insync** app) and **Dropbox** are two cloud services, both of which have apps that work well with the command line.

This book isn't going to focus too heavily on web-apps,

as I cover them extensively in my other book, "Going Chromebook," and really only intend to cover text-mode specific tools here. Just keep in mind that if you can't find a tool you need, there may be a tool on the web for your needs.

USING COMMAND LINE TOOLS WITH THE GUI

Sometimes the best tool for a job is not the one you *want* to be using. Sometimes, the GUI really is the more efficient way to do things. Drawing and graphics work are one good example. Image-intensive web development. Most heavily-visual game programming. Plus, some modern tools *only* work under a windowing system, not even making their features available from the command line. Sometimes you *need* Windows or MacOS to get things done.

The days of dumb terminals and text-based teletype machines are long past us. Nostalgia and minimalism are enjoyable, but there is a reason computers have moved past those things. If you're running a command line tool on a server with SSH, then you can do a lot of powerful things that way, but if you add that power to the best tools that a GUI system can offer, wouldn't that be better still? Sometimes, you may find yourself following a ten-step process to get something done that you could be using a different tool for and doing it in a single step.

My point is that now that you've learned how you can do just about everything in text mode, it's time to select what works best for you and use those tools alongside your Windows or MacOS software. If you've been running a command line from within a window on a Windows 10 machine, or from iTerm2 on a Mac, then you're already doing this. Terminator or Ubuntu Terminal on Linux is the same thing; you're running a terminal screen from within a GUI. That's not "cheating," that's the smart way to do it.

Go ahead and write that book in LaTeX or Markdown using Vim. Use the command-line version of Git to manage your versions. Compile it into a PDF with Pandoc or PdfTeX. But then use some graphic app such as Adobe Acrobat or Mac Preview or Evince to view the resulting PDF. This is using the right tool for the right job, and is the most efficient way to get the project done. If you can't find a command-line PDF viewer that you enjoy using, then don't do it that way. It's all about what gets things done in the most efficient and enjoyable manner.

Learn how to cut and paste from the terminal window into a graphical window. Learn how to copy files from your home directory onto the desktop of the graphical desktop. Sometimes it's easier to use Ranger to browse the file system than it is to use Windows Explorer or Mac Finder.

Just off the top of my head, here are two lists of tasks that I believe are better suited for one method or the other. You can do all these things from one "side" or the other, these are just what I find preferable; Your opinion is free to vary.

Better from the command line	Better in a graphical environment
Mutt for Email	PDF and Comic Reading
Text Editing using Vim or Emacs	Complex Desktop Publishing Layouts
Ranger/MC file operations (or just command line file tools)	Drawing and Graphics Creation
Music and Playlist creation	Games (Usually)
File backups, large-scale transfers, and "big" downloads	Web browsing

My point here is that the command line doesn't have to be a "lifestyle." It's one more tool in your arsenal of computer power. By learning the command line and some of the more useful tools, you can gain faster and more powerful ways to do things in a more customizable environment, often using less-powerful equipment. This whole concept is meant to be *fun*, not a prison sentence.

ADVANCED TOPICS

The following topics are optional, and are valuable from the command line or GUI in many cases.

First we talk about Markdown and LaTeX, two "languages" for describing text that allows for easier conversion to other formats. Generally speaking, if you are writing for ePub or HTML publishing, I would recommend learning Markdown. If you are writing for PDF or Print publishing, I'd look at LaTeX, but there is a lot of crossover between the two.

Next, we look at what are generally called "dot files." I've mentioned repeatedly that text apps are customizable, but haven't really delved into it. The dot files are where configuration information about each app is stored, and things like key mappings, color schemes, plug-ins, and most other customizations are accomplished by editing these files.

Third, I walk you through my dot file for the Vim editor. I am by no means a master of Vim, but I have done some basic customizations. I'll walk you through this file step-by-step as an example to show what kind of things *can* be done.

Fourth, I have included the full "specifications" for the somewhat-standardized todo.txt system of creating a text-based to-do list.

Finally, I have included a list of links as "Additional Resources" for further research.

MARKDOWN AND LATEX

In the GUI world, word processors are king of document creation. Microsoft Word, Apple Pages, even Google Docs make document creation visual and easy. If you've ever gotten lost in a tangle of indentions and missing bullet points in Word, then you know how frustrating those visual formats can be. Working with text is a mixed blessing. You have **total control** over every aspect of your presentation and data, but it comes at the cost of a higher learning curve. That sounds familiar by now, doesn't it?

I mentioned **Wordgrinder** back in the "Writing Tools" section. It's the closest thing to a "word processor" I know of for a text-only system. It allows you to do boldface, underlining, and a few other formatting things, but it's not anywhere near as robust or powerful as any of the GUI word processors. It is reliable and easy to learn; it may be enough for you.

On the other hand, if you do a lot of writing, or require more precise formatting, there are two very popular systems of *describing* your text formatting: **Markdown** and **LaTeX**.

Which of these you decide to learn depends on the kind of output you desire.

If you're writing for the web or for eBooks, you probably should take a look at Markdown. It easily converts to HTML and ePub formats, and it's extremely easy to learn. You can probably pick up the basics by watching a ten-minute Youtube video!

If you are writing with paper in mind, printouts or books or reports (or PDFs), you may want to look into LaTeX. LaTeX is a high-quality typesetting system; it includes features designed for the production of technical and scientific documentation. LaTeX is the de facto standard for the communication and publication of scientific documents.

As you can see from the examples that follow, Markdown is easy to read, even for someone who doesn't actually know that the material they are looking at is Markdown. It's easy to follow and easy to learn. LaTeX, on the other hand is scattered with various tags and brackets, and generally has more "overhead". That said, the overhead and complexity allow essentially unlimited flexibility with printed layouts–more books have been typeset with LaTeX than any other method since computers first became used in printing.

In my own workflow, this book was initially written in LaTeX, and once finished and proofread, I went through the entire thing and converted the whole thing to Markdown. The Markdown version was then converted to HTML (automatically through **Pandoc**) and uploaded to various sites as the eBook edition, while the LaTeX version was converted (automatically through **PDFLaTeX**) to a PDF file and uploaded as the print version. I used different LaTeX writing tools for my other books, "Going Chromebook" (ShareLatex.com) and "Going iPad" (Overleaf.com), but the essential process was the same.

Of course, both Markdown and LaTeX are simply "languages" that describe the text, much as HTML does. All of these text languages are simply text files that are edited using the text editor of your choice– Vim or Emacs, or even Nano could be used.

Markdown Example

```
Heading
=======

## Sub-heading

Paragraphs are separated by a blank line.

Two spaces at the end of
a line leave a line break.

Text attributes _italic_, **bold**,
`monospace`.

Horizontal rule:

---

Bullet list:

* apples
* oranges
* pears

Numbered list:
```

1. wash
2. rinse
3. repeat

A [link](http://example.com).

![Image](Image_icon.png)

LaTeX Example

```
\documentclass{article}
\usepackage{amsmath}
\title{\LaTeX}

\begin{document}
\maketitle
\LaTeX{} is a document preparation
system for
the \TeX{} typesetting program. It offers
programmable desktop publishing features
and
extensive facilities for automating most
aspects of typesetting and desktop
publishing,
including numbering and cross-referencing,
tables and figures, page layout,
bibliographies, and much more. \LaTeX{} was
originally written in 1984 by Leslie
Lamport
and has become the dominant method
for using
```

```
\TeX; few people write in plain \TeX{}
anymore.
The current version is \LaTeXe.

% This is a comment, not shown in final
output.
% The following shows typesetting power
of LaTeX:
\begin{align}
E_0 &= mc^2 \\
E &= \frac{mc^2}{\sqrt{1-\frac{v^2}{c^2}}}
\end{align}
\end{document}
```

CUSTOMIZATION WITH DOT FILES

Where to Find Them

Throughout the book, I've mentioned over and over just how *customizable* everything is, but I haven't touched on how to do any of that customization. Some text-based apps have drop-down menus and settings that are adjusted just like the settings in a graphically-based app. If that's the case, then you probably know how to do that already.

The more powerful method is by editing "dotfiles." These are files containing settings, variables, and fields that you can change with a text editor like Vim, Emacs, or even Nano. The files are usually named after the app itself, only they start with a period (hence "dotfiles"), and sometimes they have "rc" added at the end. Some examples might be:

.vimrc
.emacs
.muttrc
.tmux.config

.config

...and so on.

Note: The following applies to *any* variety of Linux. Windows and Mac systems running command line apps probably still use the same dot files, but they are going to be located elsewhere. Check the documentation for specific apps to see where the configuration files are stored and how to access them.

To see what I'm talking about, go to your home directory and do a **full** directory list:

```
cd ~
ls -all
```

You may need to scroll up and down to see everything, but there are going to be a number of files that start with a period. These files can be edited, changed, then saved to alter permanent settings for the apps. Note that dot files are "invisible" to the basic **ls** command, you must us the **-all** switch to see them. They may also be hidden if you use Ranger or Midnight Commander to view the directory listing.

Every app has different rules and settings, and there's no way I can explain them all (even if I understood them all). The best way to go about this is to use an app in its default state, and then as soon as you find yourself thinking "I wonder if there's a better way..." or "I wish this worked differently," then go online (or check the **man** file) and do a search for the app's configuration options. There's a very good chance there is a setting or a plugin that does exactly what you need.

As an example, I use the Vim text editor a lot, and I have modified its configuration file quite a bit. In the next section, I will go over my dotfile for Vim. Most other apps work in similar ways.

MY .VIMRC FILE

OK, to begin, the **.vimrc** file is located in my HOME directory:

```
~/.vimrc
```

When the Vim application is started, it scans the home directory (and maybe certain other locations) and looks for this file. If it isn't there, Vim runs under its own generic defaults. If it is there, it reads the files and changes its behavior according to what's in there. Here's mine (The line numbers are for your reference; the real file doesn't have those):

```
01 filetype off
02 set encoding=utf-8
03
04 execute pathogen#infect()
05 execute pathogen#helptags()
06 let g:airline_theme='jellybeans'
07
```

```
08 filetype plugin indent on
09 :let mapleader = ","
10
11 nnoremap j gj
12 nnoremap k gk
13 vnoremap j gj
14 vnoremap k gk
15 nnoremap <Down> gj
16 nnoremap <Up> gk
17 vnoremap <Down> gj
18 vnoremap <Up> gk
19 inoremap <Down> <C-o>gj
20 inoremap <Up> <C-o>gk
21
22 " Nerdtree start and toggle ,-n and ,-m
23 :map <Leader>n <Esc>:NERDTree<CR>
24 :map <Leader>m <Esc>:NERDTreeToggle<CR>
25
26 " Latex compile and preview key bindings
27 :map <Leader>u <Esc>:! pdflatex "%"
28 :map <Leader>i <Esc>:! evince
"%:t:r.pdf" &
29
30 " Spell check toggle
31 :map <F6> :setlocal spell!
spelllang=en_us<CR>
32
33 colorscheme slate
34 set nocompatible
35 set nonumber
36 set guioptions-=L
37 set guioptions-=T
38 set ruler
```

```
39 set undolevels=1000
40 :set wrap linebreak nolist
41
42 :set display+=lastline
43 :abbreviate img ![](.jpg)
```

That looks like a lot of really technical stuff, but this is actually very short by many Vim enthusiast's standards. Now, I'll go through this line-by-line and explain what's going on here.

- Line 1: *Filetype* tells Vim to detect what kind of file is being loaded and use syntax highlighting for that kind of file. I am not a coder, so I turned that off.
- Line 2: *UTF-8* is a standard character encoding type that is used for most print and e-books. It's also all I ever use.
- Line 4-5: *Pathogen* is a "plugin manager." Vim allows extensions and plug-ins that do things not built-in to the base Vim system. Pathogen takes care of loading and running the plugin scripts for me.
- Line 6: *Airline* is a replacements for the plain status line at the bottom of the screen in Vim. Mine has a nice blue color with different information than what Vim provides by default. It's not necessary, but I like how it looks. Mine uses the theme "Jellybeans," which is set here.
- Line 8: Turns plugins and indentation on
- Line 9: Vim has a thing called a "Leader Key" which allows you define keyboard combinations that do just about anything you can imagine. I

have my leader key set to the comma key. That means I can hit *comma-n* and something will happen. If I hit *comma-m*, something else can happen, and so on. It's a lot like hitting the CTRL or ALT key along with something else, but Vim has so much going on that most of the CTRL and ALT combinations have already been taken. The Leader key combinations are "all mine." We'll define these keys later in the file.

- Line 11-20: Vim is a programmer's editor, but I mostly write text files. I don't like the way Vim moves up or down and entire paragraph when I hit the up or down arrow keys. I am used to the way regular word-processors use the arrow keys, so here I have "remapped" the keys to move the way I want. In line 11, I have remapped the 'j' key to use the action normally associated with the keys 'gj'. Line 15 does the same thing for the down-arrow key. The vnoremap, nnoremap, and inoremap do the same things, but apply the changes to different modes. It's complicated, but your takeaway here is that you can remap any key on the keyboard to do anything you want. (Vim purists are now shaking their heads at this abomination, wondering why I don't just use the default movement keys).
- Line 22: This is a comment. It doesn't do anything.
- Line 23: Here's where things start to happen. This line maps the Leader Key I mentioned earlier with the 'n' key. When I hit COMMA-N, the plugin NERDTree runs. NERDTree is a file-browsing plugin used to select and load files.

- Line 24: Maps the COMMA-M combination to make the NERDTree window go away. I can use COMMA-N to select and load a file, then hit COMMA-M to make the selector go away.
- Line 26: Another comment
- Line 27: Maps COMMA-U to compile the text file on the screen to a PDF using PDFLATEX.
- Line 28: Maps COMMA-I to load the Evince PDF viewer and preview the file created when I hit COMMA-U.
- Line 31: Maps the F6 function key to turn spell check on or off.
- Line 33: There are numerous built-in color schemes you can use, or you can install your own. I use the built-in theme called "slate"
- Line 34: Has something to do with compatibility with the much older VI program. I don't need this compatibility, so I turn it off.
- Line 35: Turns line numbering off. Again, I write text, not code, so I don't especially care about line numbering.
- Line 36: In GUI mode (Windows or Mac), removes the left-hand scroll bar
- Line 37: In GUI mode (Windows or Mac), removes the tool bar at the top of the screen
- Line 38: Set ruler allows Vim to know and display which column your cursor is in.
- Line 39: Set the number of Undo levels.
- Line 40: This makes it so Vim will break a line at spaces or punctuation, but not in the middle of a word. Otherwise, Vim allows a line to go on for a very long time without wrapping to the screen.
- Line 42: For some reason, Vim does strange

things to the lowest line of the screen. This line
fixes that.

- Line 43: If you've ever used a tool like
  TextExpander, you'll like this. This line fixes it
  so that whenever I type the characters *img* it
  automatically expands that text into ""
  That's an empty placeholder for an image file
  when writing in Markdown. I never remember
  the specific characters involved, and because of
  this line I don't have to. When I want to insert an
  image, I type "img" and those characters pop up.
  Then I go back in and fill in the description and
  file name. You can set up any unique string of
  characters to expend into anything you want this
  way. I've only included this one abbreviation
  here, but it's not uncommon to have dozens
  of them.

How did I learn to do all this? I tried using the "vanilla"
Vim program, and when I hit something I didn't like, I
Googled until I found the configuration commands.
Mastering and squeezing out every last drop of power and
performance out of these tools is a serious hobby for some
people, and they love to write about their exploits online. At
the very least, you should experiment with changing the
color scheme and turning on spell check– those are easy
commands to start with. Then build things up one step at a
time. My advice is also to NOT copy anyone else's configuration files— not even mine. Make up your own as your
needs grow.

So that's my Vim file. Just about every application you
can find has something similar to this, although usually not
so elaborate or complex. If you don't see the dot file in your

root directory, look inside the ~/.**config** subdirectory; some-time they hide them in there. If it doesn't exist in either .config or in your home directory, check the documentation for the software– it almost certainly has *some method* of making permanent customizations, it's just a matter of finding the file. It's also a very good idea to keep backups of all your customized dot files. That way if you set up another machine, those files are easily available, and also if you mess something up, you can go back to the previous working version.

This may seem at first to be unnecessarily complex. Surely it would be easier to select options from a menu? Well, that's true if the choices are limited to what the creators of the program (in this case Vim), thought to include. Apps like Vim allow an *unlimited* variety of plugins and features that border on the ridiculous. There's no way the Vim programmers would have thought to include every-thing, nor would they want to. Many plugins are *very* special purpose. By using completely open text files for configura-tion settings, pretty much anything goes as far as what can be created.

TODO.TXT FORMAT

Copied from https://github.com/todotxt/todo.txt (GPL 3.0)

A complete primer on the whys and hows of todo.txt

The first and most important rule of todo.txt:

A single line in your todo.txt text file represents a single task.

Why plain text?

Plain text is software and operating system agnostic. It's searchable, portable, lightweight, and easily manipulated. It's unstructured. It works when someone else's web server is down or your Outlook .PST file is corrupt. There's no exporting and importing, no databases or tags or flags or stars or prioritizing or *insert company name here*-induced rules on what you can and can't do with it.

The 3 axes of an effective todo list

Using special notation in todo.txt, you can create a list that's sliceable by 3 key axes.

Priority

Your todo list should be able to tell you what's the next most important thing for you to get done - either by project or by context or overall. You can optionally assign tasks a priority that'll bubble them up to the top of the list.

Project

The only way to move a big project forward is to tackle a small subtask associated with it. Your todo.txt should be able to list out all the tasks specific to a project.

In order to move along a project like "Cleaning out the garage," my task list should give me the next logical action to take in order to move that project along. "Clean out the garage" isn't a good todo item; but "Call Goodwill to schedule pickup" in the "Clean out garage" project is.

Context

Getting Things Done author David Allen suggests splitting up your task lists by context - i.e., the place and situation where you'll work on the job. Messages that you need to send go in the @email context, calls to be made @phone, household projects @home.

That way, when you've got a few minutes in the car with your cell phone, you can easily check your @phone tasks and make a call or two while you have the opportunity.

This is all possible inside todo.txt.

todo.txt format rules

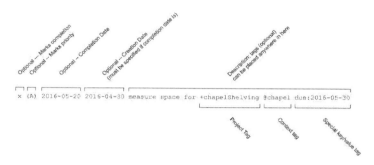

Format Quick Reference Image

Your todo.txt is a plain text file. To take advantage of structured task metadata like priority, projects, context, creation, and completion date, there are a few simple but flexible file format rules.

Philosophically, the todo.txt file format has two goals:

- The file contents should be human-readable without requiring any tools other than a plain text viewer or editor.
- A user can manipulate the file contents in a plain text editor in sensible, expected ways. For example, a text editor that can sort lines alphabetically should be able to sort your task list in a meaningful way.

These two goals are why, for example, lines start with priority and/or dates, so that they are easily sorted by priority or time, and completed items are marked with an x, which both sorts at the bottom of an alphabetical list and looks like a filled-in checkbox.

Here are the rest.

Incomplete Tasks: 3 Format Rules

The beauty of todo.txt is that it's completely unstructured; the fields you can attach to each task are only limited by your imagination. To get started, use special notation to indicate task context (e.g. @phone), project (e.g. +Garage-Sale) and priority (e.g. (A)).

A todo.txt file might look like the following:

```
(A) Thank Mom for the meatballs @phone
(B) Schedule Goodwill pickup +GarageSale @phone
Post signs around the neighborhood +GarageSale
@GroceryStore Eskimo pies
```

A search and filter for the @phone contextual items would output:

```
(A) Thank Mom for the meatballs @phone
(B) Schedule Goodwill pickup +GarageSale @phone
```

To just see the +GarageSale project items would output:

```
(B) Schedule Goodwill pickup +GarageSale @phone
Post signs around the neighborhood +GarageSale
```

There are three formatting rules for current todos.

Rule 1: If priority exists, it ALWAYS appears first.

The priority is an uppercase character from A-Z enclosed in parentheses and followed by a space.

This task has a priority:

```
(A) Call Mom
```

These tasks do not have any priorities:

```
Really gotta call Mom (A) @phone @someday
(b) Get back to the boss
(B)->Submit TPS report
```

Rule 2: A task's creation date may optionally appear directly after priority and a space.

If there is no priority, the creation date appears first. If the creation date exists, it should be in the format YYYY-MM-DD.

These tasks have creation dates:

```
2011-03-02 Document +TodoTxt task format
(A) 2011-03-02 Call Mom
```

This task doesn't have a creation date:

```
(A) Call Mom 2011-03-02
```

Rule 3: Contexts and Projects may appear anywhere in the line *after* priority/prepended date.

- A *context* is preceded by a single space and an at-sign (@).
- A *project* is preceded by a single space and a plus-sign (+).

- A *project* or *context* contains any non-whitespace character.
- A *task* may have zero, one, or more than one *projects* and *contexts* included in it.

For example, this task is part of the +Family and +Peace-LoveAndHappiness projects as well as the @iphone and @phone contexts:

```
(A) Call Mom +Family +PeaceLoveAndHappiness
@iphone @phone
```

This task has no contexts in it:

```
Email SoAndSo at soandso@example.com
```

This task has no projects in it:

```
Learn how to add 2+2
```

Complete Tasks: 2 Format Rules

Two things indicate that a task has been completed.

Rule 1: A completed task starts with an lowercase x character (x).

If a task starts with an x (case-sensitive and lowercase) followed directly by a space, it is marked as complete.

This is a complete task:

```
x 2011-03-03 Call Mom
```

These are not complete tasks:

```
xylophone lesson
X 2012-01-01 Make resolutions
(A) x Find ticket prices
```

We use a lowercase x so that completed tasks sort to the bottom of the task list using standard sort tools.

Rule 2: The date of completion appears directly after the x, separated by a space.

For example:

```
x 2011-03-02 2011-03-01 Review Tim's pull
request +TodoTxtTouch @github
```

If you've prepended the creation date to your task, on completion it will appear directly after the completion date. This is so your completed tasks sort by date using standard sort tools. Many Todo.txt clients discard priority on task completion. To preserve it, use the key:value format described below (e.g. pri:A)

With the completed date (required), if you've used the prepended date (optional), you can calculate how many days it took to complete a task.

Additional File Format Definitions

Tool developers may define additional formatting rules for extra metadata.

Developers should use the format key:value to define additional metadata (e.g. due:2010-01-02 as a due date).

Both key and value must consist of non-whitespace characters, which are not colons. Only one colon separates the key and value.

ADDITIONAL RESOURCES

Using the Linux Command Line (pdf book)
`http://linuxcommand.org/tlcl.php`

Plaintext Productivity
`http://plaintext-productivity.net/`

Inconsolation: Adventures with lightweight and minimalist software for Linux
`https://inconsolation.wordpress.com/`

SC Spreadsheet Calculator Article
`http://www.linuxjournal.com/article/10699`

SC Mini Manual
`http://www.adrianjwells.freeuk.com/minmansc.pdf`

Beamer Home Page
`https://github.com/josephwright/beamer`

Vimdeck Home Page
`https://github.com/tybenz/vimdeck`

MDP Home Page
`http://xmodulo.com/presentation-command-`
`line-linux.html`

Terminal Velocity Home Page
`https://vhp.github.io/terminal_velocity/`

Awesome Shell - A curated list of awesome command
line apps.
`https://github.com/alebcay/awesome-shell`

Git Pro book by Scott Chacon and Ben Straub and
published by Apress available for free:
`https://git-scm.com/book/en/v2`

Most Useful Command Line Tools: 50 Cool Tools to
Improve Your Workflow, Boost Productivity, and More
`https://stackify.com/top-`
`command-line-tools/`

Pass Password Manager installation and tutorial:
`https://www.2daygeek.com/pass-command-line-`
`password-manager-linux/`

CONCLUSION

And that's it. Plenty of apps and ideas to get you started and inspired. Check out the links in the preceding section, learn to browse through the main pages for the commands and apps you've installed, be on the lookout for new and updated apps, and most of all, use the right tool for the right job!

I'm sure there are important apps I've neglected to remember and important pointers that I've left out. Drop me a note by email or through Twitter or something and let me know. There will be a second edition of the book someday, and your suggestions will help make that possible.

Enjoy!

```
sudo shutdown -h now
```

ABOUT THE AUTHOR

Brian Schell is a former College IT Instructor who has an extensive background in computers dating back to the 1980s. Currently, he writes on a wide array of topics from computers, Buddhism and world religions, to ham radio, old-time radio shows, and even releases the occasional short horror tale of how own.

He'd love to hear your stories of success and failure with the command line. If there's something you would like to see in a future edition of the book, or otherwise have suggestions, please drop him a note. Contact him at:

```
Web: http://BrianSchell.com
Email: brian@brianschell.com
```

twitter.com/BrianSchell

facebook.com/Brian.Schell

instagram.com/brian_schell

pinterest.com/brianschell

ALSO BY BRIAN SCHELL

Amateur Radio

- D-Star for Beginners
- Echolink for Beginners
- DMR for Beginners Using the Tytera MD-380
- SDR for Beginners with the SDRPlay
- OpenSpot for Beginners
- Programming Amateur Radios with CHIRP

Technology

- Going Chromebook: Living in the Cloud
- Going Text: Mastering the Power of the Command Line
- Going iPad: Ditching the Desktop
- DOS Today: Running Vintage MS-DOS Games and Apps on a Modern Computer

Old-Time Radio Listener's Guides

- OTR Listener's Guide to Dark Fantasy

The Five-Minute Buddhist Series

- The Five-Minute Buddhist
- The Five-Minute Buddhist Returns
- The Five-Minute Buddhist Meditates
- The Five-Minute Buddhist's Quick Start Guide to Buddhism
- Teaching and Learning in Japan: An English Teacher Abroad

Fiction with Kevin L. Knights:

- Tales to Make You Shiver
- Tales to Make You Shiver 2
- Random Acts of Cloning
- Jess and the Monsters

Made in the USA
Columbia, SC
04 May 2022

59901737R00074